Orange Persephone

poems by

Margaret Lee

Finishing Line Press
Georgetown, Kentucky

Orange Persephone

ACKNOWLEDGMENTS

Many of the poems in this collection were born in workshops or
consultations with New Mexico poets I have met through the programs
of SOMOS in Taos. I am happy to be in the company of those indebted
to Jan Smith, its Executive Director, for creating a lively space for writing.
My thanks to Lise Goett, Valerie Martinez, David Meischen, Catherine
Strisik, and especially Sawnie Morris, an extraordinary teacher, and Veronica
Golos, whose expertise and enthusiasm apparently knows no bounds. This
chapbook barely begins to express the countless ways my two children,
Abigail and Rick, have shaped my sense of self. If heaven were a place, I
would find it only by riding their coattails.

The epigraph for "No Hiding" comes from Joy Harjo, "Break My Heart,"
in *An American Sunrise*, W. W. Norton and Company, 2019, page 3.
Translations from Sappho in "Acheron" are my own.

Publisher: Leah Huete de Maines
Editor: Christen Kincaid
Cover Art: Egon Schiele
Author Photo: Margaret Lee
Cover Design: Elizabeth Maines McCleavy

Order online: www.finishinglinepress.com
also available on amazon.com

Author inquiries and mail orders:
Finishing Line Press
PO Box 1626
Georgetown, Kentucky 40324
USA

Contents

For Abigail

Cento

Brave bloom burst—
    I labor with this curl, this fish
        black center like the sea
            fingers like the osprey's wings
                hair in seaweed strands.

            Dawnstreak at the horizon,
        my inner layers hold your shape.
      This glowing, this female light
    stolen for a season
ashy howl, endless night.

I lurched from sleep to the canyon rim
    silver line
        one-dimensional night
            the burn behind the mark you made
                I cried like autumn rain.

            Grey grief, a thousand deaths.
        Too large, too close, the pain.
      I parted your hair with my eyes.
    I know my truth—no mystery—
vast, engulfing, self-sufficient.

Waiting river, rushy surface
    beyond a child's dream
        before a woman's despair
            secret-keeper.
                Where are they, those enfolding arms?

            A garment soon to be cut from the loom.
            When, the leaf's greening?
        Say spring, say breeding, signal songs.
    This pecking thought—blind,
wet-feathered, faint.

A Wave

I took my grief to the sea
　　and the waves mirrored the spreading clouds.

Grey grief, a thousand deaths
　　and the waves curled white against the sky.

A thousand deaths, the sound when he fell, my love, on cold tile—blue
skin, faint heart, his cry
　　and the waves pounded against the cliffs
　　and the waves swallowed the spent seafoam.

I held my grief scar-gashed, poisoned, radiation-burned

　　and the waves swelled green beneath blue sky
　　and the waves crashed against black basalt
　　and the waves thundered beneath the rocks.

Memory layers, my love's only son, a candle snuffed in dead of night,
bone and shell, a thousand deaths
　　and the waves seethed through mussel flats
　　and the waves littered the beach with kelp.

I fed my fury to the steady sea
　　and the mountain shadow chased the waves.

Grey grief, a thousand deaths
　　and the sea surged beneath the waves.

The cry no one heard, my firstborn child, on suicide watch in a hospital
room, no light in her face
　　alone,
　　　　alone
　　　　　　and a veil of salt spray peeled away from the wave
　　　　　　and a kelp field floated out to sea.

Her surgery, a scalpel, lights, needles, beeping machines
    alone,
        alone
            and a wave swallowed the spotted seal
            and a harlequin duck jumped through the rapids.

I gave my cries to the tourmaline surf
    my little girl,
        my little girl,
            my little girl,
                my little girl

            and a cormorant beat its path above the waves
            and a surf scoter bobbed amid the waves

her son, her daughter, confused, alone
    and a pied billed grebe dove into the wave
kindergarten on a computer screen
    and a squabble of gulls circled the waves
party-less birthdays, long silent hours
    and a loon dove for fish beyond the waves.

The children,
    the children,
        the children,
            the children

    and the waves spread long fingers across the sand

    and the waves ferried the bobbing sea ducks

    and the waves rode the tide to shore

  a wave

        a wave

    a wave

          a wave

Mourning

When, the leaf's greening?
How can I disburden grief?
The grey dove sings it.

Love Nest

The knowledge—that your beating heart could stop—my hands cannot—conduct its rhythm—that my child's face could lose—its light—my caring cannot—heal her—that cells in my own breast—conspire to take my life—the weight of it—crisp leaves as they fall—silence—then a rustle—a pecking—a shell crack

how hope feels—
blind, wet-feathered
faint.

Kore

Daughter, answer
to every question—
orange Persephone,
the way I think
of you—
name sprung
from earth, ancient
people, distant places.

Orange, unabashed
brave bloom burst
unsubtle; evening
brilliance, burnt
edges, fire.

Secret-keeper, stolen
for a season
underground, endless
night—I cried
like autumn rain,
thundered to find
you, flooded
to flush you out
earth's birth canal
knowing, yes—
I knew you
still breathed,
you—life's definition.

Persephone, first
flowering, escape
your earthy prison—
I will hold
you, hold back
cold winter,
keep you—

but no—ever
turning earth—only
you hold
future's seeds; no
one keeps
You.

Daughter-Quake Tanka

By Sea

The break happened deep.
To stop the pain, she chose death—
an earthquake at sea—
muffled rumble, drowning waves,
ashy howl from ocean depths.

I became ocean.
My wave-tossed hands—seaweed fronds
floating slick and green
in tear-salt—caressed broken
pieces. She drifted alone.

By Land

Her voice—nightmare-tossed,
wild-eyed, went silent—swallowed
in life's noise, beyond
desperation—cold desert
of isolation. Sinking.

I heard—lurched from sleep
to the canyon rim—darkness—
darkness and her cry.
The night silence, its acid
edge, never again quiet.

I Will Wait for You

I will wait for you
here, where we met once—
a silver line in the dark—
until you return

Alone She Lies

I never had to urge her out of bed
as a child.
Her goal for today:
take a shower.
I cannot reach her.

Too large, too close, the pain.
Her children wonder when the crying
will stop, when they will see her.

In the blackened hands of a rescued miner
a wrapped rock—hard, cold memory—
gift to those who have not seen
his companion,
the inside of darkness.

How can I receive
her rock, one-dimensional night,
the only thing left
unchanged?

You Will Remember

… the day your horizon disappeared

your throat burning

invisible ants digging tunnels

your blue weighted blanket

the grey stretch every afternoon

how long an hour was

housed in silence …

… but I recall the February chill

how I parted your hair with my eyes
searched for the coral tint
along your cheekbones

the yellow paper umbrellas
I laid on tumbler rims—
apple juice, herbal tea

the muffled click—
your bedroom door-latch—
white barrier

inbreath
when I saw
the scar.

Unraveled

Is it the same—living, dying—
this web of days?

Opposing tensions—Will, Fate—
bind me in place.

I am a garment soon to be cut
from the loom.

First, Chaos
                              then Earth—
            no progenitor,   no explanation—
they   came   into   being
            vast,   engulfing,
                        feminine
            self-sufficient.

            Hesiod's   *god*
So goes   song,   *no*   *made*
                        Muse-inspired: *them.*

Behind their becoming
            stood
                  no male might, no epic story;
                  never created, never consumed,
                  not inscribed onto some
                              deep
                              void.

            Earth, alone,   **Chaos,**
                  mothered   un-
            Sky and Sea,   partnered,
                        gave   birth   to
            Mountains, home   edgeless Darkness,
                  of the gods.   blackening Night.

Birth places   first Mothers   turbulent spaces
                  womb and destiny
                        Earth, Chaos
            sisters   coequal

            vast,
                  engulfing,   feminine,
                        self-sufficient.

No Hiding

History will always find you, and wrap you
In its thousand arms.
          —*Joy Harjo, "Break My Heart"*

Where are they, those enfolding arms?
          Do they rise from the earth
          reach down from the sky?
Do they spring from the seeds of all we have done
          scatter in the winds of love and hate
          settle in the air of indecision?

Do they deliver an otherworldly fate
          the consequence of star-clashes
          air masses from earth-currents
Forces that move and mark
          our coming and going
          loving and leaving?

Wrapped in history's thousand arms
          heavy as a woolen blanket
          smothering, comforting
Encased in its shell
          protected, imprisoned
          an embrace.

Becoming "I"

Writhing amoeba
in my mirror—
grey eye-globes, sea creatures
in my mouth—not my face
but the churn that made me,
that I make.

I labor with this curl,
this fish—
belly-buried
large-headed
straining to breathe
against my becoming.

That is why
I cannot say *I*
without tugging at
my voice.
Tell me who I am.

Touch me, give me
my boundary—
now I feel the edge.

I have to feel
this edgeless birthing—
near day.

If a crocus\/
—*After Evie Shockley*

élan's palette springs from ancient deaths `'˄' the corm swells with hermaphrodite flower `'˄' I have my mother's voice `' my father's sorrow `'˄' sharp green shoot `' not from roots but bulging stem`'˄' beyond a child's dream `' before a woman's despair `'˄' surprises sheltered deep `'˄' each daughter-cormel from where the mother bled `'˄' layered petals packed tight `'˄' petal-cups draw the gaze down `' spreading snow colors `' sunbeam `' twilight `'˄' morning's purple blooms die at dusk `'˄' a winter night for my orange Persephone `'˄' her daughter's autumn efflorescence under loamy carpet `' latent saffron stigma wrapped in dead petiole sheaths `' my papery tunic enfolds `'˄'˄'

Without Using the Word

Stretched—one way to say *beyond myself,*
lured out to where a touch erases all
there is—just this sting where your skin
was next to mine, the burn behind the mark
you made, the place where you remain. Us two,
inextricable—another word
for these heathered colors, why I feel it
when you move, why I sense your absence.
Perhaps *surprised*... to find these inner places,
to hear the sentence end after yes,
to see you always as a morning child—
maturity and youth at once. To float,
let go the roots, rest in movement, re-
define these pale words, tell
their secrets.

Perception

Your azure eye—black
center like the sea
depths—there is blue.

There is green. Pale,
silver-laced, barely visible
hydrangea bud, bulge
at its base where
the leaf's broad platter
lies curled, the plan
of its future
meandering edge
enfolded.

There is red, fugitive—
black-beaked cardinal
in flight. Dawnstreak
at the horizon

       for a moment

there is yellow, corner
of the white-throated
sparrow's eye, the millet husk
she eats. Summer's
coreopsis.

A glint—
light reflected
from the river's
rushy surface, from
your eye's clear lens
that drinks the colors in,
spills them
on your mental canvas,
the picture you make—
the way you, only you,
see the world.

Confrontation

There is no self—
only many selves I own, disown—
multi-limbed, many-headed.

My inner layers
hold your shape.
In you, my imprint.

False boundary of the body,
a stand of aspen
joined underground—

I greet the self I know inside
you. Face to face
we stand.

[So far untitled]

Alone at the sea, always alone—
water hammers each memory in,
retching surges slam the basalt flats.
Buried tympani, low and deep—
my stomach-drumhead, stretched across,
your heart the mallet.

It is only I and the sea, the fizz that floats
when the salt remembers where you stepped,
mussel tips cracked by your worn shoes
when you walked out
as far as you could, before
the tide filled in
the space
between rocks.

Black rock, black water. I see
into its depth, the slick glimmer
of your wet jacket, your young hands,
fingers like the osprey's wings,
your hair in blonde seaweed strands—
the rocks remember.

You, on the horizon now,
twice your height then, holding
your own son's hand—
another sea star—
orange this time.

I smell your wet clothes,
fold sea-spray arms around you,
the vast all of you, hold you in,
alone at the sea.

Undoing

I lay it down, this pecking thought of hidden
flaws, this way of seeing from inside
as if through peepholes; squinting view, the need
to know if I have, or lack, a purpose.

The duty not to rest; to ride the fences,
scan horizons for disaster's strike;
haunting tension wringing out the sap
of joy, of wonder—now I lay it down.

I lay down the losses, empty cup
whose rim I hold, cold, its shallow depth
with traces of the joy that was decanted.
This wanting—reaching for a different life,

a face uncarved by care, a body without
scars—this doll house dream—I lay it down.

Acheron

… but this
pernicious god…
truly I did not love…
now, though, because…
and the cause neither…
nothing much…

Now that death lurks, I lust—
    a healthy body
    a hush
    a tomorrow

<< >>

having gained… mercy… trembling…
aging skin now… surrounds… flies, chasing…
violets tucked in hidden folds…

While death chases me
I run after this spring's bloom, stars
    in a roiling sky, forgiveness,
    the unwritten poem.

<< >>

I just want to be dead

Too much
to take in—
    my mistakes, broken promises,
    the lullaby I should have sung…

I want to end it—
more than that,
I want the wanting.

Reaching arms,
willow branches waving—
dew glimmers
on the lotus leaves.

<< >>

...Womanly Dawn... golden-armed...
fate ...

I confront my fate
like dawn—
gold light.

My daughter speaks
womanly

"I know my truth—
no mystery."

<< >>

... some yearning holds me in its grip... to see ...
the lotus-covered banks ....

.
.
.
.

Waiting river—
quiet glide past my past.

Note:
Stanzas in parentheses by Sappho, fragments 67A, 21, 94,
6, and 95.

I Wouldn't Have Looked Out the Window Above
—*After Mary Szybist*

the kitchen trash can today when
I threw away my coffee grounds, except this
time the window framed a house
finch perched on the blue
flagstone near scattered vermiculite and shriveled
roots of neglected seedlings I bought
last spring, just before the world broke, endless
trail of disaster—after that
I stopped looking out windows for
thin brown streaks and strawberry
colored patches on throat and forehead
that say spring, say
breeding, signal songs from all
kinds of birds.

Luminosity

As a child I chased
fireflies—hidden light
tracked with young eyes

in summer twilight, a few feet
above ground, my eye level then—
colored light from little beetles.

Where does it come from, mama?
Secret light engulfed in darkness.
Somehow I understood

this glowing, this female light—
firefly of inner twilight, lightning
of my current self, staring

into the dark.

Margaret Lee is a poet, scholar, fiber artist, watercolor sketcher, and aspiring naturalist in Tulsa, Oklahoma. She finds poems in the Oklahoma prairies, New Mexico deserts, Oregon seashores, and inner landscapes. Her previous chapbooks include *Someone Else's Earth* (Finishing Line 2021), poems built around the surviving fragments of Sappho; *Sagebrush Songs* (Finishing Line 2022), a meditation on landscapes of northern New Mexico; and *Oklahoma Summer* (Finishing Line 2023), a reflection on recent ecological and demographic challenges in Oklahoma. Her poems have appeared in *From Behind the Mask* (Paperback-Press 2020), *Echoes of Tradition* (Tulsa Nightwriters 2024), *The Atlanta Review* and *Pangyrus*.

Margaret earned a B.A. in History from Seattle University, Seattle, WA; an M.Div. from Phillips Theological Seminary, Tulsa, OK; and a Th.D. from the Melbourne College of Divinity, Melbourne, Australia. Her academic research and publications focus on the ancient Greek language and the history and culture of the ancient world.

www.ingramcontent.com/pod-product-compliance
Lightning Source LLC
Chambersburg PA
CBHW022059080426
42734CB00009B/1419